MICROSOFT
TEAMS
FOR TEACHERS

A Quick Reference Guide for Classroom Teachers, Educators and School Administrators

CATHERINE
CORLEY

Copyright

Catherine Corley
ISBN: 9798663258753
ChurchGate Publishing House
USA | UK | Canada
© Churchgate Publishing House 2020

Table of Contents

Chapter 1

Getting Started With Teams for Educators

The Microsoft Team for educators is a feature of the Microsoft 365; such that once you buy any Microsoft 365 package, you automatically have access to the Microsoft Teams for your school, staff and students at large. Because of this, we will begin by unrolling the Microsoft 365, which is the box that packs the Teams features. The Microsoft office 365 now includes Microsoft Teams for education, which implies that you and your students can now use Teams free of charge. Your school should kindly note that the Office 365 is now addressed as Microsoft 365. You should endeavor to inform your students about this change. You can sign up on the Microsoft 365 as a student, a teacher or a school administrator.

Signing up on the Microsoft 365 website as a student

The students can access the Microsoft 365 packages with their email on the Microsoft website by following these steps;

- When a student access the Microsoft 365 web @ https://www.microsoft.com/en-us/education/products/office, he/she will see a page to enter the school email address

Get started with Office 365 for free

Students and educators at eligible institutions can sign up for Office 365 Education for free, including Word, Excel, PowerPoint, OneNote, and now Microsoft Teams, plus additional classroom tools. Use your valid school email address to get started today.

Enter your school email address

| | GET STARTED |

o Once the student enters the mail address, he/she will be taken to the page below where he can choose whether he is a student or a teacher

Are you a student or a teacher?

Office 365 Education includes Microsoft Teams and other tools you need for your online classroom. Teams allows students and teachers to chat, work on assignments, and co-create documents. If you're an IT admin, sign up your school.

I'm a student ⊛   I'm a teacher ⊛

o On selecting the "I'm a student" option, he/she will be redirected to a page to verify identity by entering the country code and phone number. A verification code will be sent to the phone number

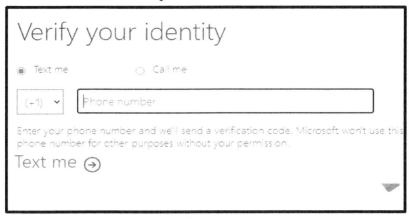

o Enter the verification code sent to your mobile and then tap the sign up icon

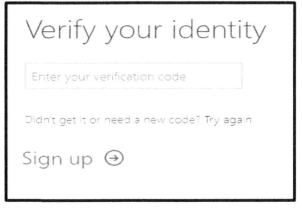

o You will be directed to a page where you are expected to create your office account as a student. Enter your names accordingly and create your unique password. You will also be prompted to enter the verification code sent to your student mail account.

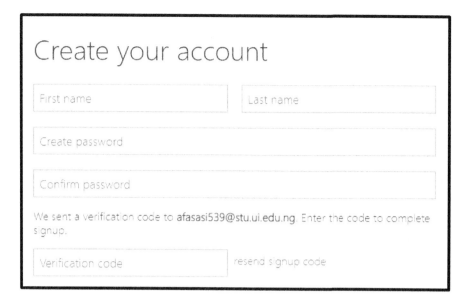

o Tap the start icon to complete registration.

Signing up for the Microsoft 365 for your entire school (As an

administrator)

Before you can sign up for the Microsoft 365 for the entire school, you need to verify that you are a verified academic institution. Follow these steps to get started;

o Copy the address https://www.microsoft.com/en-us/microsoft-365/academic/compare-office-365-education-plans?activetab=tab:primaryr1 to your web browser.

o From the website, a page will be displayed where you can register as a student and for the school. Tap the "Get started for free tab" to register for the school.

o You will be redirected to the welcome page where you are expected to fill in the following information; country, first name, last name, business mail and phone number, company's name and the size of your organization (this is the capacity of your school).

o Once you are done filling the required information, click on the "Next" icon.

o You will be redirected to a page where you are expected to choose a mail for your organization and set the password. The organization mail chosen here will be your username. The mail format will be "username @yourcompany.onmicrosoft.com." It is advisable you use the name of your school as the username. For instance, if the name of your school is Green Spring College; consider using greenspring@yourcompany. onmicrosoft. com as your school's username.

o Tap the "create my account button" to get started.

By clicking **Create my account**, I confirm that I have read and understand the Trial Agreement. If I am signing up on behalf of an organization, when I click Create my account, I represent that I have the authority to bind my organization to the terms in this agreement and that, as the representative of my organization, I agree that my organization is bound by this agreement and its linked websites.

Create my account ⊙

o You will get a page asking you to enter your organization's phone number. Tap the "text me" icon to enable Microsoft to send you the verification code.

o Enter the verification code and click "Next."

Enter your verification code

This is required.

Didn't get it or need a new code? Try again

Next ⊙

o A page will be displayed which contains the sign in page and your school's User ID.

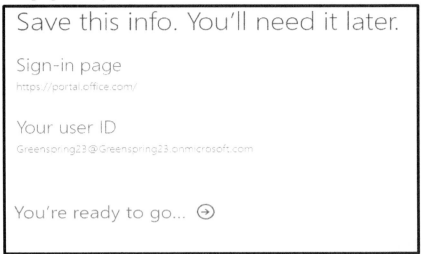

o Tap the "You're ready to go" icon and you will be taken to your organization's Microsoft 365 Admin Center, which is personalized for the school's administrator.

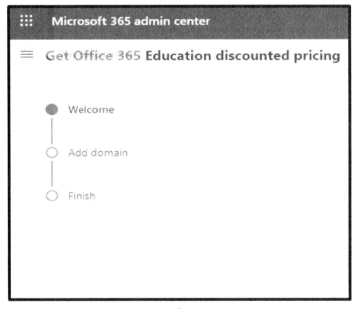

- The welcome page below is displayed where you will have access to add your school's domain. When you add your school's domain, you will be able to buy your favorite Microsoft 365 at a discounted price.

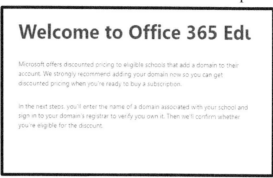

- Tap on the "Next" icon and you will be taken to the page to set up your organization's domain. Use your school's username as the domain.
- Verify the domain set up by tapping on the "Verify" button below

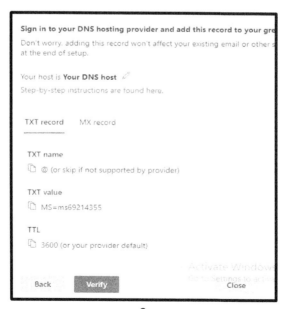

o Having set up the Microsoft 365 account as an administrator, you can then decide which Microsoft 365 plan is best for your students and teachers.

Signing up for your preferred Microsoft 365 plan as an admin

The Microsoft 365 for educators has various plans that you can choose from as a school administrator. You have the option of buying a plan for your students and staff. You don't need to worry because all the Microsoft 365 plans have Microsoft Teams embedded. The categories of plan that you can choose from as an administrator include;

1. **Microsoft office 365 A1 (for students, teachers, faculty and staff):** This office version is free and you don't need to pay for it. The only con is that it doesn't contain as much features as other office plans that you pay for, and it is only available on the web. It features popular apps such as Microsoft Outlook, Microsoft Word, Microsoft PowerPoint, Microsoft Excel and OneNote. These applications provide a platform for seamless teaching, and teachers can rely on them to share files and presentations for the students. It also integrates a lot of amazing services such as Exchange, OneDrive, SharePoint, *Microsoft Teams*, Microsoft Forms, School Data Sync, Yammer and few other interesting services. The students can leverage this Microsoft plan to work together as a team, while co-authoring and accessing the same documents. The Microsoft Teams that come with this plan can allow

students to integrate their conversation, calls and video while even when they are not within the school community. The Outlook for the web allows the students to be active with their email while giving them a 50GB mailbox space. The Microsoft Forms can be utilized by teachers to assess the whole class while giving them tests and exams, which can be submitted within stipulated time.

2. **Office 365 A3 (for students, teachers, faculty and staff):** The students' version of this plan goes for 2.5USD per month, while the version for teachers, faculty and staffs go for 3.25USD per month. It comes with all the features of the Microsoft 365 A1 version plus the desktop app and access to management and security tools. The Microsoft Publisher (for PC), and the Microsoft Access (for PC) which are absent in the A1 office plans are packed inside this Microsoft plan. The bookings service app is also included; a feature which is absent in the Microsoft Office A1 version. The students will be able to get all the values, which are included in the Microsoft Office A1 plan plus seamless installation of the Office desktop app on up to five PCs per user. The students can also install the Office apps on up to five tablets and five Smartphones per user. The mobile version is absent in the Microsoft 365 A1 plan. The teachers can also install all the Office apps on up to five PCs per user. The Microsoft Bookings that come with this plan can enable parents, guardians and students to schedule an appointment with faculty members online. The Microsoft Teams Live event

allows the faculty and staff members to hold anchors containing up to 10,000 participants.

3. **Office 365 A5 (for students, teachers, faculty and staff):** The students' version goes for 6USD per month, while the version for teachers, faculty and staff go for 8USD per month. This plan comes with all the features in Microsoft 365 A3 but the extra Microsoft's intelligent security management, advanced compliance and topnotch analytics system. The Microsoft Publisher (for PC), and the Microsoft Access (for PC), just like the Office 365 A3, are packed inside this Microsoft plan. The students will be able to get all the values, which are included in the Microsoft Office A1 plan plus seamless installation of the Office desktop app on up to five PCs per user. The students can also install the Office apps on up to five tablets and five Smartphones per user. The mobile version is absent in the Microsoft 365 A1 plan. The teachers can also install all the Office apps on up to five PCs per user. The Microsoft Bookings that come with this plan enable parents, guardians and students to schedule an appointment with faculty members online. The Microsoft Teams Live event allows the faculty and staff members to hold anchors containing up to 10,000 participants. It features unlimited personal cloud storage space, and 100GB mailbox size. The Power BI Pro included enables faculty and other staff members to access some advanced personal and organizational analytics.

Once you have subscribed for any of the plans above, you will be given the total control of the Admin center as an admin. The Admin center will give you the leverage to do all the settings for different users in your school. Let us take a look at the Microsoft 365 for educator's Admin center.

The Microsoft 365 for Educator Admin center

How to get to the Admin center: Upon signing in, make sure you toggle on "The new admin center" icon on the right hand side for full functions.

- o Sign in to your school's account using the admin log in you created. Visit admin.microsoft.com
- o Upon successful login, tap the app launcher located at the upper left and select Admin. The app launcher is indicated with an arrow in the picture below

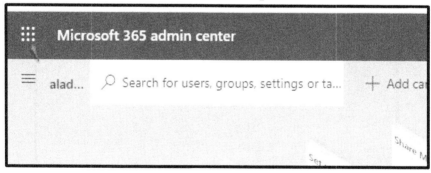

- o Be aware that the Admin pane will only be accessible if you have created your school's admin account as outlined previously.

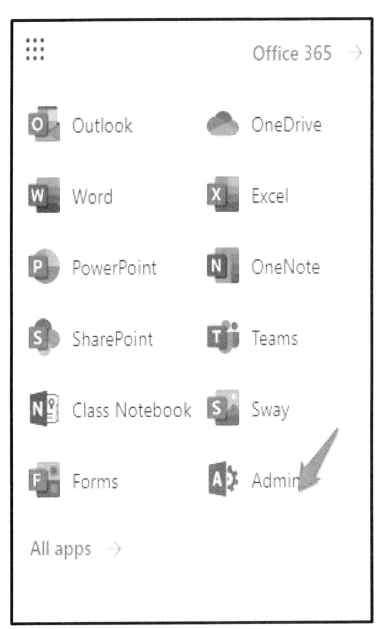

o Once you have tapped on the Admin, you will be able to have access to all the Admin features, which are located in the left navigation section of the Admin center.

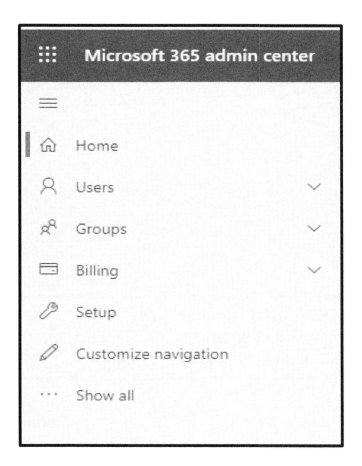

- o The menus in the admin center navigation pane are defined as follows;
- o **Home:** This is the first page in the admin center where you will have access to manage users (students, staff and teachers) in your school.
- ▪ **Users:** This is where you will be able to create and manage users in your school. Here you will see; Active users, Contacts, Guest users and Deleted users.

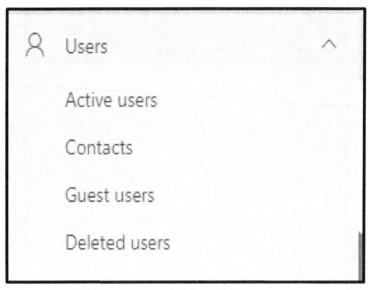

o **Groups:** Here, you will be able to create and manage groups in your school. You will have access to Groups, Deleted groups and shared mailboxes

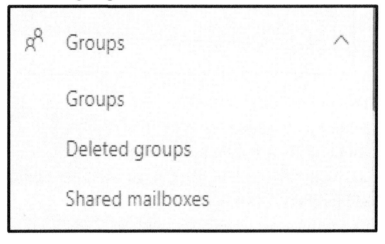

o **Billings:** Here, you can purchase services, view the services you have purchased, manage your bills and payments, assign licenses to users and check payment methods.

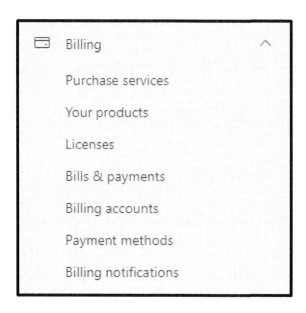

o   **Resources:** Here, you can have permission to create and manage your organization's resources such as SharePoint access collection. It features room & equipment, and the sites.

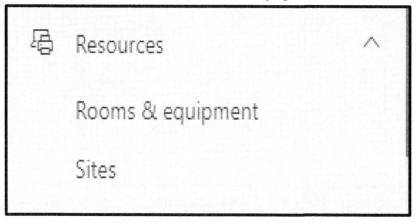

o   **Supports:** Here, you can see existing service requests or create new ones entirely.

o **Settings:** Here, you can add domains, do an org setting, search any item and view your ads-in.

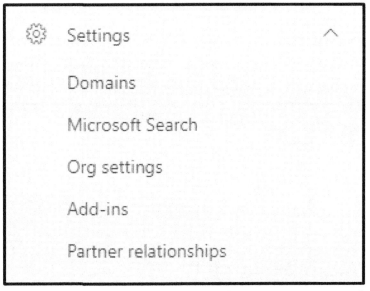

o **Setup:** Here, you can customize your custom domain setup, set passwords to never expire, limit admins to the access they need, move users' mailboxes, contacts and calendars from G-suite to Exchange Online, setup distance learning with Microsoft Teams and Get feature updates for office every month.

o **Health:** This contains; Message center to be knowledgeable of upcoming changes to Microsoft's features and services, and Service health to access the service health history and take a glance look.

o **Report:** Here, you can access how staff and students in your school are using their office account.

How to add Users

Since the Microsoft 365 Admin center has been defined, the Admin can start by adding Users. The students and staff members in your school need a user account and you can create one for them as the Administrator right from the Admin center. When you add a user, they automatically have Microsoft 365 licenses and sign in credentials.

- From the Admin center, go to *"Users"* and the tap on *"Active Users"*

o Choose *"Add a user"*

o   You will be required to fill in the following basic information about the user

o   Names: Enter the user's first name, display name, last name and the username

Set up the basics

To get started, fill out some basic information a a user.

First name

Display name *

Username *

o   Set up the user's domain: The user will be able to sign in using the domain you set up for him/her. If the user's name is Rose, and her domain is green-spring.com, then she will sign in using rose@green spring.com.

o   Password settings: You have the option of generating a unique set of password for the user or use the auto-generated password option. You can also select the ***"require this user to change their password when they first sign in"*** otherwise Microsoft will mandate them to change the password that you set for them after 3 months. The password will be sent to your mail if you choose the *"send password in email upon completion."*

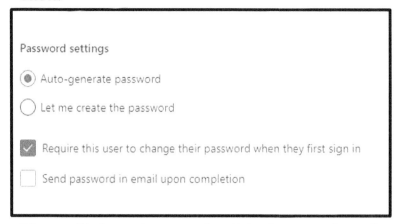

o You will be taken to the *"Assign product license"* section where you will be able to select the user's location and assign as many licenses as you want for the user. If you tap the *"create user without product license"* option, the user will have limited or no access to the Microsoft 365 features.

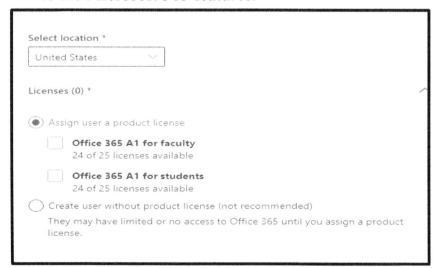

o You will be redirected to the *"optional settings"* section where you can assign admin roles to users and add additional information to users. If you select the *"Admin center access",* you have liberty to assign any admin role to any user you want. The various type of Admin roles and their functions include;

- **Exchange admin:** Full access to exchange online, creates and manages groups, manages service requests, and monitors services health.
- **Global admin:** Has unlimited access to most management features and most data in the school's admin center.
- **Helpdesk admin:** Reset password and re-authenticates password for all non-admin users and some admin roles, manages service requests, and monitors services health.
- **Service support Admin:** Creates service request for Azure, Microsoft 365 and monitors service health.
- **SharePoint admin:** Has full access to SharePoint online, manages Office 365 groups, manages service requests, and monitors services health.
- **Teams service admin:** Full access to Teams and Skype admin center, manages office 365 groups, manages service requests, and monitors services health.
- **User admin:** Reset users' passwords, creates and manages users and groups, manages service requests, and monitors services health.

Optional settings

You can choose what role you'd like to assign for this user, and fill in additional profile information.

Roles ⌄

Profile info ⌄

- Tap *"Next,"* you will be able to review the user's settings and make any necessary corrections. Select *"Finish adding"* once you are satisfied with all settings.
- Once you have successfully added the user, the Microsoft online service will send the user's username and password, and you are expected to communicate the username and password to the user.

How to assign licenses to users

You can use the **licenses page** to assign licenses for some specific products to users. You can assign licenses for up to 20 users at a time. You will be able to view the list of all the products and services that come with your Microsoft 365 packages, and the total number of subscriptions you have for each product. You can assign licenses to users from the **Active users** page or on the **License page.**

How to assign licenses to users from the license page

- From the Microsoft 365 for educator's admin center, tap on *"Billings"* and choose *"Licenses page."*

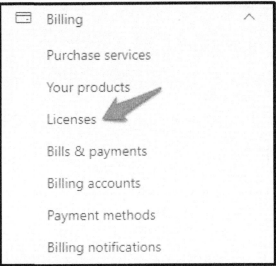

- Choose the product you want to assign licenses to

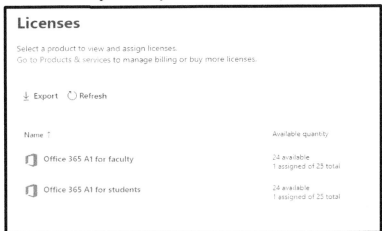

- Tap *"Assign licenses"* and you will be redirected to the *"Assign licenses to users"* section. You can type a name and add it to the list. Bear in mind that you can only add up to 20 licenses at a time, and you can only add licenses from the subscription you have bought or gotten for free from Microsoft.

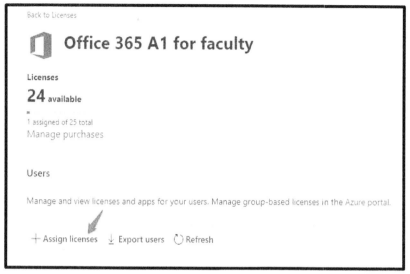

- From the "*Assign licenses to users*" pane, select "*Turn apps and services on or off*" to assign or remove any services.

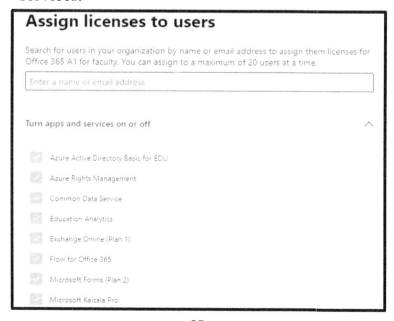

- When you are done assigning licenses, tap *"Assign"* and then *"Close"*

You can change the apps and services that you have assigned to a particular user by following these steps;

- Tap the row that contains the user's identity.
- From the right pane, select or disable selection for the particular apps and services that you want to assign or remove from the user's profile.
- Tap *"Save"* and then *"Close"* to finish.

Assigning Licenses to multiple users on the Active users page

This is used to assign licenses to multiple users. To assign licenses to users on the Active users' page, follow these steps;

- From the **Admin center,** navigate to *"Users"* and tap on *"Active users."*
- Click the circles beside the names of the users that you want to give licenses to
- Select the *"more option"* icon (…) located at the top and then tap *"Manage product licenses."*

- From the *"Manage product licenses"* section, tap *"Add to existing product licenses assignments,"* and then click *"Next."*

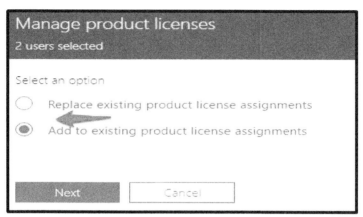

- You will be directed to the *"Add to existing products"* pane, toggle the *"On"* button for the license you want to enable for the selected user.

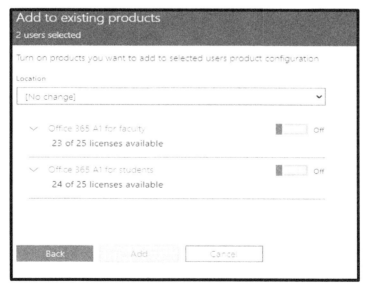

- Choose **"Add"** at the bottom and then *"Close"* to finish.

- From the **Admin center,** navigate to *"Users"* and tap on *"Active users."*
- From the *"Active user"* page, choose the row of the particular user that you wish to add licenses to
- Navigate to the right pane and choose *"Licenses and apps."*

- Click to expand the license page and choose the boxes for the license you wish to add

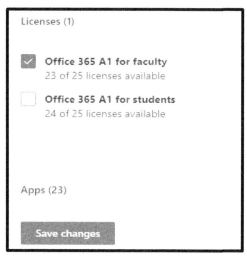

- Tap on *"Save changes"* to save selection.

How to move users to different subscription

In case you have more than one subscription, and you have already assign users to a particular subscription, you can move them to another by following these steps

- From the **Admin center,** navigate to *"Users"* and tap on *"Active users."*
- Click the circles beside the names of the users that you want to replace their licenses and subscription plan.
- Select the *"more option"* icon (…) located at the top and then tap *"Manage product licenses."*
- From the *"Manage product licenses"* section, tap *"replace existing product licenses assignments,"* and then click *"Next."*
- You will be directed to the *"Add to existing products"* pane, toggle the *"On"* button for the license you want to enable for the selected users.

- Choose "**Replace**" at the bottom and then "*Close*" to finish.

How to Unassign Licenses from users

There are two ways to remove license or unassigned licenses from users, especially if the users in question are no more working in your school or organization. Licenses can be removed on the **Active users section** or straight from the **licenses section.**

Unassign licenses from a single user using the Active users' page

- From the Admin center, navigate to *"Users,"* and tap on *"Active Users."*
- From the *"Active Users,"* choose the row of the specific user that you want to unassign licenses.
- Once you tap on the row of the user, a prompt like the one below is displayed where you can click *"Apps and Licenses."*

- Expand the *"License"* menu and deselect the boxes for the license you want to unassign.
- Choose *"Save changes"* to save selection.

Unassign licenses from multiple users using the Active users'

section

- From the Admin center, navigate to *"Users,"* and tap on *"Active Users."*
- Select the circles beside all the names that you want to unassign licenses for
- Tap on the *"More option(...)"* at the top and choose *"Manage product licenses"*

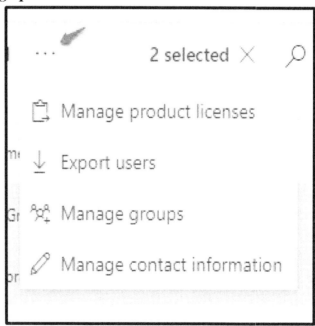

- From the *"Manage product licenses"* section, tap *"replace existing product licenses assignments,"* and then click *"Next."*

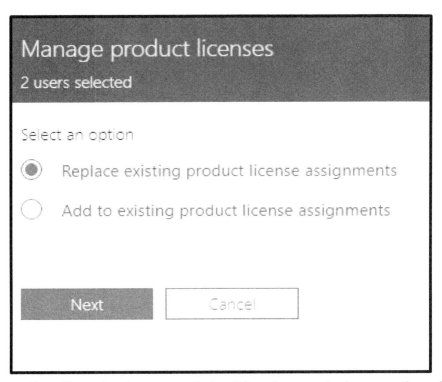

- Scroll to the bottom of the *"Replace existing products"* section, choose the *"Remove all products licenses from the selected users,"* click on *"Replace"* and tap *"Close."*

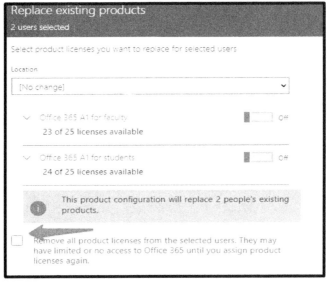

32

Unassign Licenses from users from the Licenses section

- From the Microsoft 365 for educator's admin center, tap on *"Billings"* and choose *"Licenses page."*
- Choose the product you want to unassign licenses from
- Choose all the users for which you want to unassign licenses from.
- Tap *"Unassign Licenses"* and select *"Unassign"* from the *"Unassign licenses"* boxes.

Managing Users and Groups from The Admin Center

One of the most important features of the Microsoft Admin center to understand is managing your school's groups and users right from the Admin center.

How to prevent a former employee from logging in to the Microsoft 365

If there are any staff in your school who are no longer working in your school, you need to remove them from the Microsoft 365 so that they will no longer have access to the organization's Microsoft data. To do this, follow these steps;

- From the Admin center, navigate to *"Users"* and tap on *"Active Users*
- Tap the circle next to the user's name, and then select *"Reset password"* at the top. Alternatively, you can press *"shift key + R+P"* on your computer to select the *"Select password menu"*

- Once the *"Select password"* page has loaded, select the *"let me create the password"* option
- Enter a new password and make sure you don't send this password to the user.

How to remove and delete the Microsoft 365 license from a former employee (teacher)

In order to prevent the school from paying for a license after the user has already left the school, you need to remove the user's Microsoft 365 license and then delete it from the subscription your organization is paying for. You can equally decide to assign the license to another user if you don't want to delete it. You can access the data or restore the data for the user you have deleted after 30 days. Once the 30 days limit has been exceeded, you can no longer access the data nor restore the user's data.

- From the Admin center, navigate to *"Users"* and tap on *"Active Users*
- Choose the name of the former employee that you want to block and then select *"Licenses and apps"*
- From the *"Licenses and apps"* section, uncheck the boxes for the licenses you want to remove for the user and select *"Save changes."*

How to delete a former employee's user account

- From the Admin center, navigate to *"Users"* and tap on *"Active Users*

- Choose the name of the user that you want to delete and select *"Delete user"* at the top of the name.
- Once the page is loaded, scroll to the bottom of the page and select *"Delete user."*

Restore one or more user account

If you have deleted a user, you still have 30 days to restore the user. After 30 days, the entire user's data will be permanently deleted and you will no longer be able to restore or have access to the user's data. Follow these steps to restore one or more user account;

- From the Admin center, navigate to *"Users"* and select *"Deleted users"*
- From the *"Deleted Users"* section, tap the names of the users you want to restore and then select *"Restore."*
- A prompt will be displayed where you will be able to set their password, follow the prompts displayed to set password and then choose *"Restore."*
- Once the user has been restored successfully, tap on the *"send email and close"*. Send a notification to the users that their password has changed.

How to reset my Admin password

Sometimes, as the Admin you are liable to forget your password but might be lucky to be able to login because the browser you are using has your password saved. Follow these steps to reset your password;

- Tap your name icon from the upper corner of the Admin center and select *"My Account"* from the page displayed.
- You will be taken to another page where you will select *"personal info."*

- Scroll down to the *"Contact details"* and double check whether your alternate email and phone number are correct.
- Once the correct contact details have been ascertained, tap on your name icon at the upper right hand corner and select *"Sign out."*
- After successfully signing out, you can sign in again by typing your username in the username box, click *"Next"* and choose *"Forgot password."*

- Follow the prompts displayed next to reset your password. The prompt will want to verify that you are the right person by using your alternate contact information.

How to reset password for everyone in your school at the same time

The steps below work if the staff in your school are in tens and not in hundreds or thousands.

- From the Admin center, navigate to *"Users"* and tap on *"Active Users*
- Select the circle next to *"Display name,"* to select everyone in your school. Then undone selection for yourself by tapping on your name to deselect the circle. This is because you can't reset your password as the Admin at the same time you are resetting other people's password.
- Tap *"Reset password"* or press *"Shift key +R+P"* on your computer as a shortcut.
- The *"Reset password"* page will be prompted, tap on *"Let me create the password"* to have the liberty of assigning the password that you want.
- Scroll to the bottom of the page and tap *"Reset."*
- Enter an email address to be able to receive the new password. Inform the account user of this change.

How to set the password expiration policy for your school

- From the Admin center, navigate to *"Settings"* and you will be directed to the Settings page. Note: If you are using the new admin center, turn it off to be able to access the old admin center. This will allow you to access the settings that contain the *"Security and privacy"* section.
- Select *"Security&Privacy."*
- From the *"Password expiration policy"* tap on the *"Edit"* button at the right corner.
- A page will be displayed where you can toggle on the *"Set user passwords to never expire."* You will get the option to set the number of days until passwords expire. Tap *"Save."*

Managing Groups Guest Access

You can enable or disable guest from accessing your Microsoft 365 group by following these steps;

- From the Admin center, navigate to *"Show all"* and tap on *"Settings"* from where you can have access to the *"Org settings."*
- A *"Services"* tab will be prompted next, scroll down and choose *"Microsoft office 365 Groups."*
- From the Microsoft office 365 Groups, you can choose whether to let group members outside your organization access the group's content or to let group owners add people outside your organization.

How to add a group from the Admin center

- From the Admin center, go to *"Groups"* and you will be taken to the Groups page
- From the Groups page, select *"Add a group."* Or you can alternatively press *"Shift key +A+G."*
- A page will be displayed where you will be prompted to select the Group's type that best meets your organization's needs. Select the *"Office 365"* type and scroll to the bottom to tap the *"Next"* button.
- A page is displayed where you will enter the Group's name and the Group's description. Tap on *"Next."*
- A page will be displayed where you can assign the Groups owner. The Groups owner you assign can add or remove any Group's member, and can also delete Group's conversation.
- Enter the Group's owner email and tap *"Next."*
- Another page will be prompted where you can set the Group's privacy. You can choose between **Public(anyone can see the group's content)** and **Private(Only members can see the group's content)**
- Tap on *"Finish"* and select *"Create groups"* at the bottom.

How to change a user's email address

You must be a Global Admin to effect these changes

- From the Admin center, navigate to *"Users"* and tap on *"Active Users."*

- Choose the user's name and select *"Manage username"* from the *"Account"* tab.
- A page is prompted requesting you to enter the new email address for the user. You can also enter an alias for the user – which is another email address that people can use to message the user.
- Tap *"Save changes"* when you are done.

How to change a user's display name

- From the Admin center, navigate to *"Users"* and tap on *"Active Users."*
- Choose the user's name and select *"Manage contact information"* from the *"Account"* tab.
- A display name box will appear where you can type a new name for the user, and then *"Save."*

How to add guests to a Microsoft 365 groups from the Admin center

- From the Admin center, go to *"Groups"* and you will be taken to the Groups page
- Select the groups that you want the guest to have access to and choose *"View all and manage members"* from the *"Members"* tab.
- Click *"Add members"* and select the name of the guest you want to add
- Tap *"Save."*

How to edit a group's name or description

- From the Admin center, expand the *"Group's"* menu and then select *"Groups."*
- Choose the Group that you want to edit and then tap *"Edit name and description."*
- Update the name and write a new description for the group, and then tap *"Save."*

How to manage Groups owners and members

- From the Admin center, expand the *"Group's"* menu and then select *"Groups."*
- Tap the name of the Group that you want to manage to have access to the settings pane.
- From the *"Members"* tab, decide if you want to manage owners or groups.
- Tap *"Add"* to add a person to the group or click the "X" button to remove a person from the group.

Send copies of Groups conversation to Groups members' inboxes

- From the Admin center, expand the *"Group's"* menu and then select *"Groups."*
- Tap the name of the Group that you want to manage to have access to the settings pane.
- From the *"Settings"* tab, choose *"Send copies of groups conversation and events to groups members."*
- Tap *"Save."*

Let people outside the school email the group

- From the Admin center, expand the *"Group's"* menu and then select *"Groups."*
- Tap the name of the Group that you want to manage to have access to the settings pane.
- From the Admin center group list, select the name of the group that you want to effect, and then choose *"Allow external senders to email this group"* from the *"Settings"* tab.

Chapter 2

Getting Started With Teams for Educators

Microsoft Team for educators is an all-important communication-based workspace rolled out with the Microsoft 365(formerly Office 365). With Teams, educators can share files, teach and provide needed assistance to students and other staff while working remotely. Teams bring your organization together under one goal - which is to work as a Team while prioritizing organization's aims and objectives. With Teams, you can;

- Coordinates projects, tasks and share content with the usual workplace applications that you are familiar with
- Get updates about what is happening in your school even when you are not in the school environment or you are on holiday.
- Collaborates with other staff and educators that are not in your school through Team's seamless information transfer.

Your organization does not need to worry about where to get Teams, as the Microsoft 365 for Education now comes with Teams. This means that once you subscribe to any of the Microsoft 365 for education plan, you automatically get the Teams package.

Get started with Teams for your class (as educator and as student)

Signing in to Teams (as educator)

- Tap to open your favorite web browser (Chrome, internet explorer or Mozilla Firefox) and visit

www.office.com. You will be required to sign in with your school email and password.
- Once the page has loaded, tap the **Teams** app to open.

Signing in to Teams as a student

- Tap to open your favorite web browser (Chrome, internet explorer or Mozilla Firefox) and visit www.office.com. You will be required to sign in with your school email and password.
- Once the page has loaded, tap the **Teams** app to open.
- Click **Teams** at the left corner of the page to check which class Teams you are in. You will be able to see the class Teams that you belong to if your teacher has created a Team and added you.

Creating a class Teams

The teacher will not be able to create a class Team unless the permission has been granted by the Microsoft 365 Group admin. The admin will make the teacher a Teams owner. The person that creates the Teams is assigned the Teams owner by default. The Teams owner can create and delete Teams at will. Follow these tips to successfully create a class Teams;

- Click on Teams ⚙ icon from the left hand corner of the Teams interface.
- The *"Join or create Teams"* page will pop up where you can either choose to *"Create a Teams"* or *"Join Teams with code."*

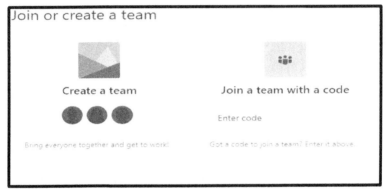

- The *"Select Team type"* page will be prompted where you can choose the type of class you want to create. Tap the first category, which is *"Class"* Teams.

- Enter the name for your Teams on the page that will be displayed after selecting the Teams type. You can also provide a description for your class, which is optional. Click on *"Next."*
- Note: If you can't see the option to create a Team on your Teams for education interface, kindly contact your school's IT Admin to give you the permission to create a class Teams.

Adding students and teachers to your Class Teams

- You can add a student to your class Teams by searching for the student's name on the *"Search for students"* bar, which will be displayed just after creating the class. Adding students to your class Teams is optional at this stage and you can skip this stage if you don't want to add students yet.
- You can also add a Teacher to your class Teams by searching for the teacher's name on the *"Search for teacher"* bar, which will be displayed just after creating the class. Adding teachers to your class Teams is optional at this stage and you can skip this stage if you don't want to add teachers yet.
- In the case that your school has already created a class group, you can contact the school's Admin, ask for the names of the class, and manually enter them. This will make your work simpler and faster.

Getting your Teams organized will help you to easily find and assemble your Teams conversation, class assignment, class files and notes that are essential for the smooth running of the class.

- **The Class Channel:** Every class Teams you created comes with a **General channel.** The Teams channel helps you to organize your conversations, class files and class apps all in one place for easy accessibility. The **General channel** features the following tabs

    o **The post tab:** this is where you see all the messages in the channel.
    o **The files tab:** this is the tab where all the files in the channel are being stored.
    o **The Class notebook tab:** this tab stores the class notebooks for the Teams.
    o **The Assignment tab:** this tab is used for creating assignments.
    o **The grades tab:** for monitoring students' grades.

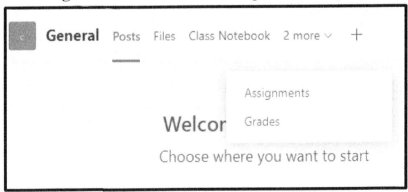

o   **Tips For the students:** the **Post tab** is the tab where you and your colleagues can chat and reply to conversations with your teachers. The **Files tab** is where you will be able to access all the documents shared by your teacher and colleagues. The **Class notebook tab** stores the class notebooks for the Teams. **The Assignment tab** is used for assessing assignments. **The grades tab** is for monitoring your grades.

- **Adding channels**
  o You can add a channel by selecting the *"More option"* beside the name of the class, and then choose *"Add a channel."*

o   Provide the name and the channel description for the channel you want to create.

o   You can also select *"Privacy"* for your channel. This is where you will be able to choose whether you want your channel to be accessible to everyone on the team (standard) or to be accessible only to some specific group of people in the team (Private). The class's name is **Chemistry** and the Channel's name is **Physical Chemistry.**

o   You can check the box at the bottom so that the channel can start showing automatically on everyone's channel list.

o   Tap *"Add"* to finish.

Communication in the Class team (for educators and students)

-    **How to create and respond to messages in Teams:** Follow these tips to message your class

o   Tap on **Teams** ⚄ to write a message for the whole class, and then pick the specific class team and channel you want to write to.

o   Tap on the *"Post tab"* to start conversation.

o   Scroll to the bottom of the *"Post tab"* and you will see a section (bar) where you can write your message.

o   Write the message and click on *"send"* ▷

o   You can notify all the class members of your new post by using @ followed by the name of your class.

-    **Starting a conversation with one student or a group of students in your class**

o   Select the *"New chat* ✎ *"* icon at the top of the Teams app. The new chat icon is found at the left side.

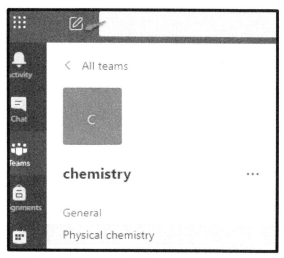

- Enter the name(s) of the student(s) you want to message inside the *"To"* field.

> To: Enter name, email, group or tag

- Write your message inside the compose box at the bottom page and tap send.

- **Replying to a conversation**
  - Find and select the specific conversation thread you want to send your replies to.
  - Tap on *"Reply,"* write your message and select *"Send."*

- **Making an announcement:** you can call your students attention to an important message by making use of the Teams announcement feature.

- o Choose *"Format "* located at the bottom of the *"compose a new message"* bar.
- o Tap *"Announcement"* and choose a background color suffice to reinforce the importance of the post you want to make.

- **Using stickers and emojis**
  - o Select *"Stickers* located beneath the *"Compose box"* to choose from any of the stickers which have been customized for you.
  - o Choose *"Emojis"* to send smiley faces and *"Giphy"* to use any of the animated GIFs.

- **Scheduling a virtual meeting for the class.**
  - o Tap on *"Teams"*, and then choose *"Calendar"*
  - o Tap the *"+ New meeting"* icon at the top of the page.

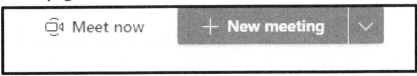

- o A page will be prompted where you can assign a name for the meeting, add required attendees for the meeting, set the specific date, and time that you want the meeting to take place.
- o Choose the *"Add channel"* to have access to the list of your class teams and their respective channels, and then select the specific channel you want to meet in.

o Tap *"Send"* to finish.

Assigning presenter permission during meeting

- Click open the *"Meeting option"* from your calendar
- Assign presenter permission by using the "*Who to present dropdown.*"

The teacher can intimate the student about the dos and the don'ts of the meeting before the commencement of any meeting. This is to ensure that there is no disturbance during the meeting. The teachers can include the following guides in the meeting invitation they send to students;

To join the online lesson;

- Click the *"Join using Microsoft Teams"* embedded in the body of this email.
- Mute your device's microphone and turn off your video when joining the meeting.
- Tap the *"Join button"* to join the meeting.
- Tap the *"Chat button"* to open the chat.
- Write *"Hand Up"* in the chat to raise your hands during the meeting.
- The teacher will turn on your microphone for you when he/she is ready to answer your question.
- Follow rules as you would in the normal class settings.

How to adjust your views in Teams meeting

Sometimes, you might want to shift your attention away from the meeting just for a brief period, follow these guides to tell your teams;

- **Switching between people and contents in Teams:** When someone is sharing a content or presentation during the meeting, you can maneuver between viewing the content and your colleagues in the meeting room by tapping on the video or the presentation you have interest in.
- **Pinning a video:** right-click on any video you want to pin during the meeting and choose *"Pin."* You will still be able to view the video regardless of who is currently making the presentation. You can right-click on any video and tap *"Unpin"* anytime you want.
- **Reframing a video:** Sometimes, the video you are watching may be too wide and Teams will need to crop the video to better fit your device's screen. You can change this setting by right clicking on the video and then choose *"Fit to frame."* You can crop the video to have a closer view by right clicking on the video and selecting *"Fill frame."*

Instructions to improve the effectiveness of the online meeting

- The teacher can consider mapping out how he/she will begin the class with the students. Do you have the right modalities in place to run an effective online class? Will you allow video in your online meeting? Will you allow students to chat with one another during the meeting? Do the students need to signify their interest to ask a question by typing *"hands up"* in the chat?

- If the students are new to online class, the teacher can help them by providing them with the following meeting etiquettes;
  - o No other face timing that is different from the intention with which the class was established.
  - o Any students who refused to follow the laid-down guides will be removed abruptly from the meeting.
  - o Students might block their background if video is allowed in the meeting.

Recording an online class meeting

Recording a meeting can be important to serve as a point of reference to the teachers and the students. Recording a meeting will create a transcript and closed captions that are searchable within the chat. Immediately the meeting has started, you can record any meeting by tapping on *"more option"* and selecting the *"Start recording"* button.

Leaving an online class meeting

The students or teachers can leave the online class meeting when they are done by tapping on the ***"Hang up"*** button.

How to change or set meeting policy for the school as an

administrator

The Admin has the permission to set meeting policies that will determine what features are available to participants and the meeting organizers. Some of these policies include;

- Permission to allow or disallow cloud recording during the meeting.
- Permission to turn on or turn off IP video.
- Permission to turn on or turn off screen sharing mode.
- Permission to turn On or turn Off the white board feature during meeting.
- Permission to turn On or turn Off the Shared note feature during meeting.

The Admin can follow these guides to change or create a meeting policy

- Navigate to the Microsoft Teams admin center, tap on ***"meetings,"*** and select ***"Meeting policies."*** Choose any policy from the list available or you can create or add new policy entirely. Add a name and description for the policy if you are creating a new policy. The name should not be longer than 64 characters and special characters are not acceptable.

- Tap *"Save"* to finish.

Assigning a meeting policy to one user

- From the left navigation section of the Microsoft Teams admin center, click on *"Users"* and then select the specific user that you want to assign the policy to.
- Choose the user by clicking to the left of the username, and then select *"Edit settings"*
- From the *"meeting policy"* section, choose the policy that you will like to assign and then select *"Apply"* to apply the policy for the user.

Assigning a policy to multiple users at one time

- Navigate to the Microsoft Teams admin center, tap on *"meetings,"* and select *"Meeting policies."*
- Choose the specific policy you want to assign by tapping to the left of the policy's name.
- Choose *"Manage users"* and search for the user name. Choose the name of the user and then tap *"Add."* Repeat the same procedure for the next user that you want to add.
- Tap *"Save"* to finish.

The school administrator can also do the following settings on behalf of the school;

- Permission to allow or disallow anonymous users to participate in the meeting.
- Permission to create customized meeting invitations.

How to allow anonymous users to join the Teams meeting

Turning on the anonymous join will allow anyone to join the meeting anonymously.
- Navigate to the Teams admin center and tap *"Meetings>Meeting settings"* from the left navigation pane.
- Under the *"Participants"* page, turn on the *"Anonymous user can join the meeting"* option.

How to customize meeting invitation

- Navigate to the Teams admin center and tap *"Meetings>Meeting settings"* from the left navigation pane.
- Enter the following settings under the *"Email invitation"* page that will be prompted;
  o **Logo URL:** Type in the web address where your school logo is stored.
  o **Legal URL:** Type in the address if your school possesses any legal webpage that people can access for legal issues.
  o **Help URL:** Enter the web address of your school's support center.

- o **Footer:** Type in the text that you want to appear in the footer.
- Tap the *"preview invite"* to see how your meeting invitation looks like. You can correct any wrong information.
- Tap *"Save"* to finish.

Meet with students using the video or audio call

- Click on the *"New chat"* located at the left hand side and then type in the students names inside the *"To"* box.
- Tap *"Video call"* to use the video meeting or tap the *"Audio call"* to use the audio meeting.

Joining and managing a meeting

- Tap on *"Calendar"* and go to the meeting you wish to join.
- Open the meeting and choose *"Join."*
- Turn on your device's camera to be seen and un-mute your device's microphone to be heard.
- Tap the *"Join now"* to enter into the meeting space.

Sharing and organizing files in Teams

As a teacher: Any files or document that you shared in the channel or chat will be seen by all the students.

- Inside your channel conversation, tap on *"Attach"* located under the box where you used to type your message.

- Once the *"Attach file"* has loaded, you can select from one of these options; Recent, Browse Teams and Channels, OneDrive and the Upload from my computer option.

- Select any file and choose *"Share a link."* If you are selecting a file from your computer, select the file to open and tap on *"Send ▷"*

- Any file you shared will be stored in the *"Files tab."*

Adding class materials

This can be used to add any important document that you don't want the students to edit.

- Scroll to the *"General channel"* of your class team.
- Tap the *"Files tab"* and select the *"Class materials folder."*
- Choose the *"Upload"* option to add the file from your computer or OneDrive.

Assignments and grades in your class Teams

Create Assignment

- Scroll to the *"General channel"* of your class team and click on the *"Assignment tab."*
- Click on *"Create>Assignment."*

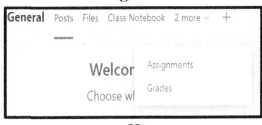

- You can decide to add details to the assignment you give to your students. Details such as Title (required), Choose multiple classes or individual students in one class to assign to, Add additional instructions, add resources, Select a due date and time, Points available, Add a grading rubric and Add a category.
- You can add more resources by;
    - Tap *"Add resources"* to select from the existing files or you can decide to create a blank Microsoft 365 document and then assign it to each student.
    - Choose the *"Attach"* button. The default mode for the file is *"Students can't edit"*. What this means is that your students cannot edit the resources that you are sharing; they can only read them. You can change this setting so that students will be able to edit and turn in the assignment by selecting *"more option..."* and choosing *"Students edit their own copy."* This will send an identical copy of the file to all the students and they will in-turn be able to edit and submit the assignment.

Choosing deadline for the assignment

- Tap the *"Edit button"* under the due date to determine whether you will accept late submission from your students or not.
- Tap *"Done"* to finish.

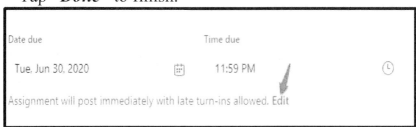

Viewing Grades: you can deploy the View grades tab to monitor your students' progress and access their grades.

- Scroll to the *"General channel"* of your class team and click on the *"Grades tab."* Assignments appear in rows and each student's name will appear in a column. Assignments are arranged by due date, with the nearest date at the beginning. Move down or across to continue viewing assignments.
- The following statuses are assigned to each student's assignment;
  - **Viewed:** this indicates that the student has seen and opened the assignment.
  - **Turned in:** this means that the student has submitted the assignment and you can now grade it.
  - **Returned or points:** this shows the point you assigned to each student's assignment after grading.
  - **Blank:** this means that you have not yet taken action on the student's assignment.

Grading turned in work

- Tap on the *"More options…"* on a cell to *"Open student work."*
- By tapping on *"opening student work,"* you will be able to fill in the *"Feedback"* and *"points"* field.
- You can write comments on the document itself by tapping on the *"Edit document,"* and then choose between editing in the desktop app or the web browser.
- Choose *"return"* when you finished grading the assignment and you want the student to receive it.
- You can return multiple assignments at once by;
  - Tap on the *"Assignment tab."*
  - Choose an assignment.
  - You will be able to enter each student's feedback and points without necessarily opening the student's work.
  - You can use the check-boxes to choose the names of the students you want to return their assignment.
  - Tap *"return."*

How to setup class notebook as an educator

Class notebook affords the students the opportunity to take note and share knowledge effectively among them.

- Scroll to the *"General channel"* of your class team and click on the *"Class notebook"* tab. Then tap *'Setup a OneNote Class Notebook."*
- Follow the setup instructions.

Navigating your teams in Teams

- Tap the ***"Teams"*** icon at the left navigation bar to display the list of teams where you are a member.

- The teams that you used often will be displayed at the top of the view. You can view the rest of the teams not in display by tapping on ***"Hidden teams"*** at the bottom of the page. You can rearrange the teams order by selecting and dragging them around.

- Tap the ***"More Options…"*** tab on the team card to edit settings for a team.

- You can view the team members by tapping ***"Manage teams"*** and then select ***"Members."***

Switching to list view for teams

- Click on ***"Teams."***

- Tap the ***"More Options…"***  icon beside the ***"join or create Teams"***

- Click on *"Switch View."*
- The *"Layout"* section will be prompted where you are expected to select *"List."* This will change your teams view from Grid to List view.

More about teams and channels in Teams

Teams are groups of people that assemble under a common goal and objective within an organization. Inside **teams**, there are **Channels**, which are the conversation framework that take place within the teams. Each **channel** describes a specific topic or assignment at hand. The **channels** are actually the powerhouse of the team where tasks are carried out. The **channel** is the place where the team members get to chat, have either audio or video conversations, sharing of files and where apps that are essential for the teams are added. The conversations in the **channels** are available for all the group members, but **private chats** are between the two parties that are chatting – no other person is privy.

Teams owner, Members and guests capabilities in Teams

Every Teams member has their roles and permission within the group.

- **Teams Owner:** Teams owners have certain advantages, which an ordinary teams member cannot have. Team owners can add and remove any team member and change some specific settings. The team owners are also assigned the permission to add and remove guests. They also carry out specific administrative functions for the team.

Specifically, the team owners have the following capabilities;

- **Create a team.**
- **Participate in a private chat**
- **Participate in a channel conversation**
- **Share a channel file**
- **Share a chat file**
- **Add apps (such as tabs, bots, or connectors)**
- **Create a team**
- **Delete or edit posted messages.**
- **Discover and join public team**
- **View org chat**
- **Add or remove members and guests**
- **Edit or delete a team**
- **Set teams permission for channels, tabs and connectors.**
- **Change the team's picture**
- **Control @ [team's name] mention.**
- **Allow use of emojis, GIFs and memes**
- **Archive, renew and restore a team**

- **Teams Members:** the team members are the people in the team who do not have the type of liberty bestowed. The team members can upload files and converse normally within the team. The team members have the following capabilities;

- **Create a team.**
- **Participate in a private chat**
- **Participate in a channel conversation**
- **Share a channel file**

- Share a chat file
- Add apps (such as tabs, bots, or connectors)
- Create a team
- Delete or edit posted messages.
- Discover and join public team
- View org chat

- **Guests:** These are individuals that are not members of the school. They are neither students nor teachers in the school. They are usually added by the team owner to participate during the team session. They don't have as much capabilities as the team members or team owners. The guests have the following capabilities;
  - Create a team.
  - Participate in a private chat
  - Participate in a channel conversation
  - Share a channel file
  - Can be invited via any work or school account.
  - Delete or edit posted messages.

Manage Teams settings and permission

- Navigate to the team's name and tap on *"More options..."* then select *"Manage teams."*
- Check or uncheck the permissions you needed from the *"Settings tab"*

▸ **Team theme**	Pick a theme
▸ **Member permissions**	Enable channel creation, adding apps, and more
▸ **Guest permissions**	Enable channel creation
▸ **@mentions**	Choose who can use @team and @channel mentions
▸ **Team code**	Share this code so people can join the team directly - you won't get join requests
▸ **Fun stuff**	Allow emoji, memes, GIFs, or stickers

Change team's name, permission and privacy settings

- Navigate to the team's name and tap on *"More options..."* then select *"Edit teams."*

Viewing Teams analytics for all of your teams

You can check the activity details of any teams that you created or that you are a member of. The information you will obtain can include; the number of active users, the number of guests, and even the total number of messages that have been sent in the team so far.

- Tap on *"Manage teams"* located at the downside of your team list

68

- Select a date range that you want to view usage data on the *"Analytics tab."*

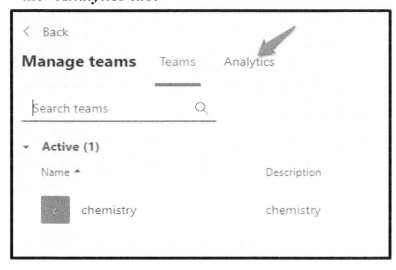

Viewing team analytics for an individual team

- Select the team that you need, tap on the *"More options..."* and select *"Manage team."*
- From the *"Analytics tab,"* choose the date range for the specific team you want to its usage data.

Show, hide or pin a team or channel in Teams

- **Show a team or channel (on desktop)**
Any team that you are a member of will be automatically displayed on your team lists. If you don't see a particular team that you belong to right on your team list, it is possible that the team has been hidden. Simply move to the bottom of your team lists and choose *"Hidden teams,"* find the team that is hidden by choosing *"More option..."* and then select *"Show."*

- **Show a team or channels (on iOS)**

  Any team that you are a member of will be automatically displayed on your team lists. If you don't see a particular team that you belong to right on your team list, it is possible that the team has been hidden. Scroll to the bottom of your team list and choose *"See all teams."* You can also show any hidden channel by selecting *"Teams"* and then move to the bottom of the team list. Click on the *"See all teams"* at the bottom of the team list, then choose the team that the channel is in. select the circle beside the channel you want to show. You can hide it by tapping the circle again to deselect.

- **Hide a team or channel on desktop**

  Scroll to the team or channel's name, and tap *"More options…"* then tap *"Hide."* You can also show channels from the **hidden channels** menu beneath the channels list of a team. Select "**More options** ⋯ > **Show.**"

Pinning or Unpinning a channel

Pinning a channel ensures that the channel stays at the top of your channel list and you don't have to worry about looking for it whenever you need it. To pin any channel, scroll to the channel's name and click *"More options…"* then choose *"Pin."*

Deleting a team channel

To delete any channel, scroll to the channel's name and click *"More options…"* then choose *"Delete this channel."*

Customize channel notifications in Teams

To customize notifications for any channel, scroll to the channel's name and click *"More options…"* then select *"Channels notifications."* This gives you notifications about any channel activity. The below are the customizable settings that you will see in channels notifications;

- **All new posts:** this will tell you anytime a user begins a new conversation in the channel.
- **Include all replies:** this will tell you anytime a user replies to a conversation that has already been initiated.
- **Channels mentions:** this will tell you whenever a user @mention the channel.

Using @ to get someone attention in teams

You can use @ together with a name to get someone's attention in a channel conversation or a chat. By just typing @ right in front of their name, you can get anyone's attention in chat. The persons you @ will receive a notification that will lead them to the conversation where their names have been mentioned and they can actively attend to the mention.

You can get the attention of the whole team by doing any of these;

- Post a notification in the Teams general channel. The channel's name will be boldly displayed for every member of the teams.
- Write @**teams** to get everyone's attention in the team.
- Write @**Channel** to get the attention of everyone who used to frequent the channel.
- Note that the team owner must have these features enabled before any user can deploy them.

Using tags in Teams

With tags, you can reach a group of people all at once. You can categorize people in your team based on professions, attributes, locations, roles or training. For instance, a Nurse or a Doctor tag will enable you to reach out to diverse groups in teams without necessarily having to type their names out. Once you have created a tag, just @mention the tag's name in a channel and everyone under the tag will receive the notification just as if they would receive it if they have been mentioned individually.

Creating and managing tags in teams.

- Tap to select *"Teams*ᵉᵗᵒᶾ *"* on the left navigation pane and scroll through the lists displayed to find your team.
- Tap *"more options…"* and select the *"manage tags"* icon.

@**mention a tag in your channel**

You can @mention a tag in your message and choose the tag from the list displayed right from the channel conversation.

The tag will come up in the conversation just like any @mention and the people in the tag will be duly notified.

Using tags in chats

You can start a chat with the members of the tags by tapping *"New chat icon"* in Teams. Type the name of the tag and then choose the tag from the list. Everyone in the tag group will be added to the **To: field.**

Managing settings for team owners

- Team owners have the liberty to decide which member gets to add tags. Tap to select *"Teams⚙"* on the left navigation pane and scroll through the lists displayed to find your team. Tap *"more options…"* and select the *"manage tags"* icon.
- Choose the **settings** tab and then scroll to the **tags section** where you can control who gets to add tags.

Chapter 3

More about Teams

How to create a team from scratch

Follow these steps to create a team from the scratch;

- Tap on *"Teams icon"* located at the left navigation pane, then tap *"Join or create teams"* which can be found at the bottom of the teams list.
- Tap on the *"Create teams"* which is the first card located at the top left side.
- Select *"build a team from scratch"* once the create teams page has loaded.
- Select the type of teams you want to create. You can choose between **Public (anyone in your school can join)** and **Private (which will restrict files and conversation and allow them to be seen only by some specific groups)**
- Provide a desirable name for the team you have created and add an optional description for the team.
- Tap on *"Create"* to finish.

Inviting people to the team as the creator

As the team creator, you can invite people to your team by adding them. You can add up to 5000 people to your new team. Follow these tips;

- Navigate to the team name from the team list and tap *"More options…"* then select *"Add members."*
- You can begin by typing a name, security group, distribution list or Microsoft 365 group so that you can add them to your team. Add people that are not working

in your organization as guests by typing in their email address.

- Tap *"Add"* when you are done adding members to your team. You can make anyone of the team members the team owner by tapping the down arrow beside the word **Member.**
- Tap *"Close"* to finish. All the people you have added to your team will be notified and your team will start appearing on their team list.

Accepting or denying pending request

You can accept or deny pending request as the team creator by following the tip below;

- Navigate to your team from the team list and tap *"More options…">Manage teams>pending requests."*

Request to add a member

You can, on behalf of someone, request to be added to a team which you are a member of. Scroll to the team from your team list and then tap *"more options…>Add member."* Enter the name of one or more people that you want to add and then choose *"Send request."* The team creator will be notified of an impending request to join the team.

Creating a team from an existing team

You can bring the same settings, data and channels from an existing team to establish a new team by creating a copy of the old team. You can then decide how your new team will be customized.

- Tap on *"Teams icon"* located at the left navigation pane, then tap *"Join or create teams"* which can be found at the bottom of the teams list.
- Tap on the *"Create teams"* which is the first card located at the top left side.
- From here, select "**Create from…**," and then click **Team**. You will be able to see a list of teams that you own currently.
- Choose the specific team that you have decided to copy.
- Provide a suitable name for the new team, add the necessary team description and modify the team's privacy settings. Deploy the checkboxes to select which section of the teams you want to copy. Sections such as tabs, channels, settings and team apps can be copied.

Renewing a team

Team will usually notify you when the team you created is about to expire. The expiration usually appears when there is a red expiration icon next to your team's name. The red expiration icon implies that the team will expire in the next thirty days. To renew your team, navigate to the team's name and select the *"More option…"* icon. Choose *"Renew now"* from the *"More option…"* icon. Alternatively, you can navigate to the team's name and select the *"More option…"* icon then choose *"Manage team."* Then tap *"settings>Team expiration."* From here, you can select *"Renew now"* or confirm the date that your team will expire.

Creating a link for joining team

- As a team owner, navigate to the team's name and tap *"More options..."* then scroll down and select *"Get link to team"*
- Copy the link and forward the link to the person that you want to invite to the team you created. The person can tap the link and join your team meeting.

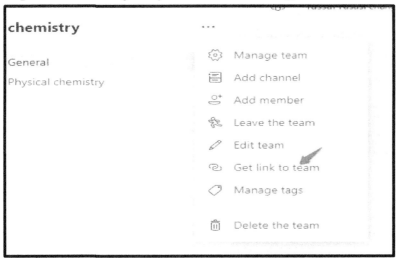

Creating a code for joining team

- As a team owner, navigate to the team's name and select the *"More option..."* icon then choose *"Manage team."*
- Click the *"Settings tab>Team code>Generate."*
- The code will be displayed and you can then copy the code to share with anyone you want.

Follow these tips to set guests permission for channels in team;

- Tap on *"Teams icon*⁣⁣⁣⁣" located at the left navigation pane. Navigate to the team's name and tap *"More options..."* then scroll down and select *"Manage team"*

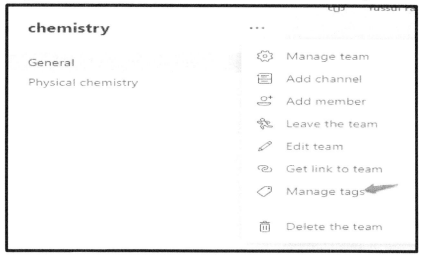

- Tap *"Settings"* and select *"Guest permission."*
- Tick or untick permission that you want to assign to guests.

Choosing a theme for Teams

- Tap on *"Teams icon*⁣⁣⁣⁣" located at the left navigation pane. Navigate to the team's name and tap *"More options..."* then scroll down and select *"Manage team"*
- Tap *"Settings"* and select *"Team theme."*
- Select the *"Change theme"* icon at the bottom.

Guests' collaboration with team members in channel

As a guest, you can join in the team conversation, mention people in the chat and edit group files.

- **To reply to a message:** tap *"Reply ↩,"* write your message and click **Enter** to send.

- **To like or save a message:** tap the *"Like 👍"* beside a message to confirm your likeness for the message. Tap the *"Save 🔖"* to save a message for a later date.

- **Get someone's attention in the channel:** you can write @ in front of a member's name to mention them in the conversation. The member will get a notification when you @ them. The Admin must enable this setting before you can use it.

- **See where you have been mentioned in conversation:** check the circle next to **Teams** and **Activity** to confirm how many times your name has been mentioned in conversation.

- **Co-edit a file:** if a team member uploads a file in the conversation, you can open the file by clicking on the file. Tap *"Edit"* and then choose where to edit the file either in the app or online. Tap the *"Message"* icon to continue with the conversation while you are still editing the file.

Chapter 4

What is New in Teams?

There have been recent additions and modifications to the Teams interface. Some of these additions make Teams more interesting and compete with other educational platforms.

June 26, 2020

- **Meeting and meeting chat size increased to 300:** The recent increment in the number of people who can participate actively in team meetings will enable more active collaboration between students, teachers and faculty members. The number of attendees that can attend the team meeting has now been increased to 300.
- **Access notification settings from Activity:** You can have quick access to notification settings right by tapping **Activity>Settings** and then select what team's activities you want to be getting notifications for.

June 19, 2020

- **Improvement in meeting in Safari:** You can now join meetings using the Safari browser on your Mac computer without Teams mandating you to deploy the Audio Conferencing to dial into meetings. The latest improvements now deploy your device's built-in microphone and speakers for speaking and listening.

June 15, 2020

- **Meet now or later in Teams free:** the free version of Teams now allows you to schedule a meeting for a later date.

June 9, 2020

- **Privacy for people joining teams via mobile phones:** To increase user privacy for users joining a Teams meeting by dialing in via phone, Teams now hides your number from any user that is not working in your organization. Your mobile number will still be visible to members of your school or organization.

May 27, 2020

- **Meeting option button in Teams:** Immediately you send your online meeting invitation, you can open your meeting options using the new button in Teams. Just tap to open the meeting event and select **Meeting options** (located right at the top of the event). This will open a tab for you in your web browser where you will be able to adjust your meeting settings, like lobby bypass and who can present.
- **Book appointments and online visits with booking:** with the introduction of the booking app in Teams, scheduling virtual appointments like an education office hour is now quite easy.
- **Pop out a chat for multitasking:** Double-click on any chat from the chat list or click ⬏ to open any chat in the secondary window. This will allow you to navigate Teams even when you are in many chat conversations.

May 15, 2020

- **Raise your hands in a meeting:** if you have any question or comment that you want to pass but you don't want to interrupt the meeting unnecessarily, you can let people know you have a question to ask with the new raise hand feature in Teams. During a meeting session, select the 🖐 located in the control bar. This will display a gold hand icon on your video feed to tell the rest of the participants that you would like to comment or ask a question.

- **Roll call:** Meeting creators can now take attendance during a Teams meeting. To download your attendance report, tap Show participants > Download attendee list. The report will be downloaded as a CSV file that can be accessed in Excel. The file will include the identity (name), the time of joining, and leave time of those that attended the meeting. May 13, 2020.

- **Meetings are now going 3x3 on desktop:** Teams promised, on this date, to start enabling up to nine(9) video streams at a time in meetings users joined using the desktop app. This will be rolled out gradually to everyone, and will be accessible in the teams meeting.

May 1, 2020.

- **Teams now feature channel analytics:** Teams now feature channel metrics being rolled out with team analytics. Together with this addition features new metrics such as a running tally of posts and replies for each team and channel. Team has also increased the time period for data to three months. Navigate to your team from the team list and tap *"More options …>Manage teams>analytics."*

- **Add system audio to Live events:** Just like in Teams meetings of the past, you can now add your system audio when making a presentation in a live event. As at the moment, this addition is only available for presenters and producers that are joining from the Teams desktop app for Windows.

April 20, 2020.

- **Let attendees who dial in bypass the meeting lobby:** You can configure settings to always allow callers to immediately join your next Teams meeting without necessarily having to wait in the meeting lobby. By so doing, you won't necessarily have to stop in the middle of a meeting session to allow participants to enter the meeting. To get this setting, click **Meeting options** and tap the toggle to **Yes** for **Always let callers bypass the lobby.**

April 17, 2020.

- **Announce when caller joins or leaves a meeting:** The person that organizes the meeting can now announce when any caller joins or leaves a Teams meeting. This enables other members to know who are present in the online meeting. To access this setting, tap **meeting options** and turn on **Announce when callers join or leave.**

April 10, 2020.

- **End the meeting for everyone:** As the meeting organizer, you now have the opportunity to end your meetings for all participants. If you're a teacher, for instance, this is a good opportunity to make sure your students don't hang around in your virtual classroom after you've deserted the meeting. To end a meeting that is in progress, scroll to the meeting controls and tap **More options** ⋯ > **End meeting**. You'll be mandated to confirm. When you confirm, the meeting will come to an end for everyone right away.

March 20, 2020.

- **Improvement to the Teams calendar:** Right-click an item from the calendar to pull up RSVP options, initiates a chat with meeting participants, or immediately joins a meeting when it starts. Team has also made improvements to the event scheduling form.
- **Work offline in the Windows desktop app:** Access and create messages in teams, even when your internet connection is slow or completely out of reach. All of your Pinned chats and channels, together with channels that you have viewed previously will also be accessible while offline.

March 6, 2020.

- **You can now create tags in Teams:** Team creators can now create tags and equally assign participants to them. With this feature, you can easily @mention a group, people, department, etc. Team owners can try this out by themselves by navigating to any team on their list, tap **more options** ⋯ and select **Manage tags**.

February 28, 2020.

- **You can now edit the content of your post:** Sometimes, you might have shared or posted an announcement to multiple channels, and later noticed that you had forgotten a channel unattended. Or you found a typographical error in the recent announcement you wrote for your school or organization. You need not fear, because now you can modify your cross-posts. Just like you would edit a single channel post, navigate to **more options** ⋯ and tap **Edit** to modify the content of the post you shared and add or remove channels.

February 21, 2020.

- **You can now pin your favorite apps:** You can now organize your apps on the left navigation pane of Teams to suit the way you work. Tap the three dots located on the left side of Teams, right click the app icon you would like to pin, and choose **Pin** to add it to your favorite for easy access.

January 28, 2020.

- **Message Read Receipts now included:** Now, sending message out to someone will get you a Seen ⌃ confirmation to the right of the message which implies that the person has read your message. By default, read receipts are automatically turned ON for every member of the group and will show in group chats with up to 20 members. Your admin has the liberty to turn this feature on/off anytime he/she wishes.

Chapter 5

Managing Phone Numbers for Your Organization in Teams

The Microsoft Teams provide four ways by which teams users can get subscriber (User) and service (toll and toll-free) phone numbers. These include;

- Obtaining a new user phone number from the Microsoft Teams admin center.
- Obtaining new service phone number from the Microsoft Teams Admin center.
- Transfer or port your former phone number
- Utilize a request form for a new phone number.

NOTE: Your school will not get the **Voice> phone number** feature included in the Microsoft 365 Admin center if you are using Microsoft subscription that is not any of these;

- **EDU A1 or A3 plan and Microsoft 365 Business Voice**
- **EDU A5 plan, which includes voice features.**
- **You can as well buy an EDU A1 or A3 plan and Microsoft 365 Business Voice and then add voice features individually.**

Once you subscribe to any of the plans above, you automatically have the voice feature enabled on the left navigation pane of your Microsoft 365 Admin center.

Obtaining new user phone number using the Microsoft Teams

Admin center

- Navigate to the Microsoft Teams Admin center at www.admin.microsoft. com.

- At the left navigation pane of the admin center, navigate to **Voice** and tap **Phone numbers.** Then select **Add.**
- Input a name for the order and write a description.
- Carry out the following actions on the Location and Quantity page which will be prompted;
  - o Choose your **country and region** appropriately.
  - o Under the **number** type section, choose **User (Subscriber)**
  - o Choose your **Location** under the **Location section.** You can create a new location if your location is not available by tapping **Add a location.**
  - o Choose an **Area code** under the **Area code section.**
  - o Enter the quantity of phone numbers you desired for your school under the **Quantity** section and tap **Next** to choose numbers.
- Click all the numbers that you want. Be reminded that you have only 10 minutes to choose and place your order. If you take more than 10 minutes, the phone numbers that you have selected will be returned to the pool of numbers you chose them from.
- Tap **Place order** to place your order when you are done.

Obtaining new service number for your school

- Navigate to the Microsoft Teams Admin center at www.admin.microsoft .com.

- At the left navigation pane of the admin center, navigate to **Voice** and tap **Phone numbers.** Then select **Add.**
- Input a name for the order and write a description.
- Carry out the following actions on the Location and Quantity page which will be prompted;
  o Choose your **country and region** appropriately.
  o Under the **number** type section, choose the **type of service number** that you want.
  o Choose your **Location** under the **Location section.** You can create a new location if your location is not available by tapping **Add a location.**
  o Choose an **Area code** under the **Area code section.**
  o Enter the quantity of phone numbers you desired for your school under the **Quantity** section and tap **Next** to choose numbers.
- Click all the numbers that you want. Be reminded that you have only 10 minutes to choose and place your order. If you take more than 10 minutes, the phone numbers that you have selected will be returned to the pool of numbers you chose them from.
- Tap **Place order** to place your order when you are done.

Create a port order and transfer your existing phone number to

Teams

Note: The steps highlighted below only work in the USA, UK and Canada at the moment. Other countries can get phone numbers by manually submitting a port order.

- Navigate to the Microsoft Teams Admin center at www.admin.microsoft.com.
- At the left navigation pane of the admin center, navigate to **Voice** and tap **Phone numbers.** Select **Numbers** and then tap **Port** to begin the porting wizard.
- Go through the information prompted on the **Get started page** and tap **Next** when you have understood them.
- The **Select Location and number** page will be prompted and you are expected to input the following;
  - **Country or region:** Choose the country or region where you are getting the phone numbers.
  - **Phone number type:** Select the type of number that you want. You can choose between geographical or toll free numbers.
  - **Number assigned to**: Select what the numbers are assigned to. You can choose between users, conferencing or voice features.
- The **Add account information** page will be prompted where you are expected to complete the following and then tap **Next;**

- o **Order details** which include;
  - ▪ **Name of your order**
  - ▪ **Notification email(s):** You will be prompted to enter an email address where you will receive your order notification. You can enter more than one email address here but only ensure you separate them by a comma.
  - ▪ **Transfer date:** the transfer date that was issued by your current service provider.
- o **Phone number details** which include;
  - ▪ **Port type:** You can opt in for a full port to transfer all of your numbers or a partial port to transfer some of your phone numbers.
- o **Person requesting detail:** input the name of your organization and the contact information of the person that is asking for the transfer.
- o **Current provider's detail:** this include;
  - ▪ **Billing telephone number (BTN):** Your BTN in E.164 format, which affords a + sign to come before the number. For instance, if you are in North America, use +1XXXYYYZZZZ format.
  - ▪ **Other details, which will include the name of your current service provider, your service address and your account number.**
- The **Add number page** will be prompted, tap **Select a file,** browse through and choose the CSV file that has the phone number you want to transfer and then select **Next.**

- The **Complete your order page** will be displayed, select **Upload a signed letter of authorization** to enable you upload a duly signed copy of letter of authorization. If you have not yet downloaded and signed the letter of authorization, do the following:
  - o Tap **Download the template** to download the letter of authorization, which is specific for your country or region.
  - o Print the letter of authorization.
  - o Let the person who is authorized to make changes to the account sign the downloaded letter of authorization.
  - o Scan the letter of authorization that has been signed, and then select **Upload a signed Letter of Authorization** to have it uploaded.
- Recheck all the details you have entered and then tap **Submit.**
- You can check the status of your order by navigating to the Admin center and then tap **Voice.** Select **port orders** and click **Order history.**

View the phone numbers for your organization

- Navigate to the Microsoft Teams Admin center at www.admin.microsoft. com.
- At the left navigation pane of the admin center, navigate to **Voice** and tap **Phone numbers.** From here, you can access the phone numbers for your school, including location, type of phone number and status information.

Microsoft Teams adopts various telephone number types, which are dependent on the intent for which you have decided to utilize the phone number for. Teams adopt **user** numbers, which is usually assigned to users in your school or organization, and **service** numbers, which are normally given to services in your school or organization such as Audio Conferencing, auto attendants, or call queues. Service phone numbers possess an increased concurrent call capacity than user numbers. Service phone numbers are usually available but normally vary by country/region and the category of number (can be a toll or toll-free number). If your organization or school requires additional or other categories of number types that are not available in the Microsoft Teams Admin center, you should tender a phone number request to the PSTN service desk help.

- **User numbers**

User numbers are normally given to users, and it is of two types:

○ **Geographic numbers:** Geographic numbers have a connection to a known geographic area and are the most available. For instance, geographic phone numbers in most instances can only be utilized within a certain jurisdiction, city, state, or region of the country.
○ **Non-geographic numbers:** Non-geographic numbers are national numbers that do not have any connection to a geographic area within a country/region. For instance, non-geographic numbers usually cost the same when calling

from any jurisdiction within your country or region. Also, there are some countries in the world that only have non-geographic numbers available.

- **Service number**

Service numbers are obtainable in various number types, and presence essentially varies by country or region. It includes;

o **Toll service number** which usually incurred a cost to the caller. It is of the following categories;
  o **Geographic numbers:** Geographic numbers have a connection to a known geographic area and are the most available. For instance, geographic phone numbers in most instances can only be utilized within a certain jurisdiction, city, state, or region of the country.
  o **Non-geographic numbers:** Non-geographic numbers are national numbers that do not have any connection to a geographic area within a country/region. For instance, non-geographic numbers usually cost the same when calling from any jurisdiction within your country or region. Also, there are some countries in the world that only have non-geographic numbers available.
o **Toll-free service numbers** These service numbers do not ordinarily incur a toll cost to the caller. Team makes national toll-free numbers available in over 60 countries or regions of the world.

Searching for phone numbers for users

You cannot assign phone numbers for users without knowing the phone numbers that are available for you in your area. To do this, use the **Get new numbers** section to look for new numbers that are available within the jurisdiction. You can carry out the search by country basis, type of number or location and then enter the quantity of phone numbers that you will require for the users in your organization. Follow these tips to look for phone numbers for your school;

- Navigate to the **Microsoft Teams admin center.**
- At the left navigation pane of the admin center, navigate to **Voice** and tap **Phone numbers.** Then choose **Get new numbers.**
- The **Select Location and quantity** page will be prompted and you are expected to choose a location from the displayed country drop-down list.
- Choose your preferred **Number type** from the displayed **Number type** drop-down list.
- The **Location box** will be prompted and you can type the name of the city the user is located and then choose the location from the displayed list. Select **Add a location** if your preferred location is not available in the drop-down list.
- Choose the area code for the selected location.
- Enter the quantity of phone numbers you desired for your school under the **Quantity** section and tap **Next.** Be reminded that you have only 10 minutes to choose and place your order. If you take more than 10 minutes, the phone numbers that you have selected will be returned to the pool of numbers you chose them from.
- The **Get number page** will be prompted where you can choose the phone numbers that you desired. Tap

Acquire numbers when you are done choosing and tap **Next.**

- A **confirmation page** will load where you can confirm the choices you have selected and then tap **Place order.**
- When you get back to the Phone numbers page, choose the phone number or numbers that you desire to assign and then tap Edit to give it to a user.

To see a list of phone numbers that you have acquired for your organization

- Navigate to the **Microsoft Teams admin center.**
- At the left navigation pane of the admin center, navigate to **Voice** and tap **Phone numbers.**
- Tap the **Status column** to access the phone numbers that are assigned
- You can filter your view by tapping the filter icon. Utilize the drop-down list on the drop-down list to filter your view by;
  o Specific number range that you have set. Searching can be done by lowest number or highest numbers.
  o Numbers that begin with a number that you have already specified.
  o Number activation state.
  o The type of phone number.
  o The status of phone number.

To see all the phone numbers that have been assigned to a specific user

- Navigate to the **Microsoft Teams admin center.**
- At the left navigation pane of the admin center, navigate to **Voice** and tap **Phone numbers.**

- Tap the **Status column** to sort the numbers quickly so that you can know which numbers have been assigned.
- You can filter your view by tapping the filter icon and then filter the view to access the phone numbers that have been assigned to users, or list of numbers that are unassigned which can be assigned eventually to a user. You can filter using; **Assigned to users, assigned to conference bridge and unassigned.**

To see the list of phone numbers that have been assigned voice users

- Navigate to the **Microsoft Teams admin center.**
- At the left navigation pane of the admin center, navigate to **Voice** and tap **Phone numbers.**
- Tap the **filter icon** to enable you to filter your view by **Activation state.**

Assign a phone number to a user

- Navigate to the **Microsoft Teams admin center.**
- At the left navigation pane of the admin center, navigate to **Voice** and tap **Phone numbers.**
- Choose an unassigned number from the list of numbers on the **Phone number page** and then tap **Edit.**
- In the **Edit** section, under **Assigned to**, look for the user by his/her display name or user name, and then tap **Assign**.
- You can assign or change the related emergency location, under **Emergency location**, by searching for and then selecting the location.
- You can decide to send an email to the user either with their phone number details or not by turning on or

turning off *Email user with telephone number information*. This is usually turned on by default.

Changing a phone number for a user

- Navigate to the **Admin center**
- Tap on **Users** from the left navigation pane of the **Admin center**, then find, and double-click the specific user you want to change number for. Select **Account**, and then take a record of the phone number that has been assigned to the user under **General information.**
- At the left navigation pane, navigate to **Voice** and tap **Phone numbers.**
- On the **Phone numbers page**, choose the number that you have already taken record of, and then select **Edit.**
- In the **Edit** section, under **Assigned to**, tap the **X** button to remove the user's number and then tap Save.
- Select an unassigned number from the list on the **phone number page**, and then tap **Edit.**
- In the **Edit** section, under **Assigned to**, look for the user by his/her display name or user name, and then tap **Assign**.
- You can assign or change the related emergency location, under **Emergency location**, by searching for and then selecting the location.
- Tap **Save.**

Removing a phone number from a user

- Navigate to the **Admin center**
- Tap on **Users** from the left navigation pane of the **Admin center**, then find, and double-click the specific user you want to remove their phone number. Select **Account**, and then take a record of the phone number that has been assigned to the user under **General information.**

- At the left navigation pane, navigate to **Voice** and tap **Phone numbers.**
- On the **Phone numbers page**, choose the number that you have already taken record of, and then select **Edit.**
- In the **Edit** section, under **Assigned to**, tap the **X** button to remove the user's number and then tap Save.

What is to come in Teams

On June 30, 2020 the Microsoft company released an article on their website telling users about the caller ID Policies they are about to unroll. So if you do not have the caller ID policy in your Team, be assured that it works in progress. Nonetheless, we can still talk about the Caller ID policies in Teams and how to manage it.

Managing Caller ID policy in Teams.

You can deploy the caller ID policy to show an alternate phone number for people in your organization or block an incoming call from displaying a number. For instance, when users in your organization make a call, you can set the caller ID to display your organization's main phone number instead of the users' phone numbers. You can manage caller ID policies for your organization by navigating to **Voice** and tap on **Caller ID policies** in the Microsoft Teams admin center. You can also deploy the global (Org-wide default) policy or set and assign custom policies. People in your organization will automatically be assigned the global policy unless you create and assign a custom policy.

Creating custom ID policy

- From the left navigation pane of the Microsoft Teams Admin center, navigate to **Voice** and tap on **Caller ID policies.**
- Select **Add.**

- Enter the name and the description for the policy.
- Start selecting the policies that you want to set;
  o **Block incoming caller ID:** Turning on this setting will block the caller ID of any incoming call from showing.
  o **Override the caller ID policy:** When you turn this setting on, users are permitted to decide whether to show their caller ID or not.
  o **Replace the caller ID with:** You can set the caller ID to be showing for users by choosing one of these options;
    ▪ **User's number:** This will show the user's number
    ▪ **Service number:** You can set a service number to be displaying as the user's caller ID.
    ▪ **Anonymous:** This will be showing the caller ID as anonymous.
  o **Replace the caller ID with this service number:** You can select a service number to replace the caller ID of users. This option is only available if you picked **Service number** in **Replace the caller ID with**.
- Tap **Save** to finish.

Editing a caller ID Policy

- From the left navigation pane of the Microsoft Teams Admin center, navigate to **Voice** and tap on **Caller ID policies.**
- Choose the desired policy by clicking to the left of the policy's name. Then tap **Edit.**
- Replace the settings that you want to change and then tap **Save.**

About Author

Catherine Corley is a software expert who has spent more than 7 years of her career consulting for organizations on basic hardware and software. Catherine is also a passionate teacher who runs an online community where she teaches a group of people on basic hardware guides and has written several instructional manuals.

Catherine holds an Msc degree in Computer engineering from University of Toronto, Ontario Canada. She is happily married with a beautiful daughter.

Printed in Great Britain
by Amazon